Christmas
Craft Party

We've included dozens of quick & easy holiday projects, decorating ideas and recipes inside.

Invite some friends, get out your crafty supplies and whip up some munchies... you'll be ready in no time to have a Christmas craft party!

★ Craft Party Basics ★

Crafting is always more fun with friends...we've made it so easy to host a party of your own!

★

Here are the basics: Pick 3 or 4 crafts that you and your friends would like to do and invite 8 to 10 friends.

★

Decide if you'll be providing supplies or organizing a crafty potluck where everyone contributes supplies they have on hand. Once you've decided, gather the supplies for each craft and make sure you have MORE than you'll need for your guests. (Someone's bound to want to start over!)

Make one of each project so your guests have a finished (and cute!) sample to look at while they craft. ★

On the big day, whip up some refreshments for your guests and set up a table or two with the appropriate supplies grouped together. Decorate the table with some Christmas cheer and be prepared for glitter to go everywhere!

★

One last thing to remember: The recipes and crafts inside may need to be adjusted depending on the number of guests you have and how many of each project they'd like to make & take...just adjust your shopping lists accordingly.

Crafty Countdown ☑

☑ One month beforehand...
Start looking for neat new craft ideas to make with family & friends. Check out your favorite books and magazines...we've given you lots of ideas inside!

☑ Three weeks before...
Send out invitations requesting RSVP's within 2 weeks.

☑ Two weeks before...
Decide which crafts you'll be doing and make a list of supplies you'll need. Choose appetizers and treats for the menu and jot down a grocery list.

☑ One week before...
Enjoy shopping at the craft store and, once you get home, make up your samples and easy instruction sheets.

☑ The day before...
Whip up any appetizers you can make ahead of time and store in the fridge. Separate all your supplies into groups by project, if you like.

☑ On the big day...
Set up individual work stations for each project you plan to make. Be sure to set out your finished example at each station along with copies of the instructions and all the materials needed. Crafters can come in and get right to the fun!

☑ Once guests arrive...
Turn on the Christmas music and sing along with your favorites. Be sure to serve up plenty of munchies and drinks to keep those crafters energized! By the time your guests head home, they're sure to be in the holiday spirit.

Just copy and color these invitation inspirations, add them to your own cardstock and personalize!

Friends will be lining up to RSVP!

Let's
get CRAFTY

Date: _____

Time: _____

Place: _____

_____

_____

_____

Spruce up invitations
with teeny tiny buttons,
stick-on foil stars or
a sprinkling of glitter!

Join us for a night of
Holiday Crafts!

✦ Theme Ideas ✦

 Put a new spin on holiday crafts with these easy ideas for theme parties. Choose one and carry it through or choose a few for a variety of projects!

Sweets

Try making ribbon-candy ornaments or candy wreaths with friends. Create a pretty party centerpiece..just fill a vase with peppermints and anchor a white pillar candle inside.

Make an easy garland! Simply lay out 6 feet of plastic wrap and then cut in half lengthwise. Place colorful Christmas candies about every 3 inches. Roll the plastic wrap over and tie ribbon or homespun between each sweet bundle.

Just the Girls

Gather a gaggle of girlfriends and make some girly goodies. You can whip up a selection of pampering gifts like lip balm and bath salts, dainty doily snowflakes sprinkled with glitter and some yummy friendship tea.

For little girls, dress up barrettes with treasures from the button box. Just hot glue the buttons on to completely cover...what a great stocking stuffer!

For a
Good Cause

Make stacks of unsigned holiday cards and tags with some friends. Donate them to local nursing homes and let someone else send your handmade greetings!

Crates of crafts can be donated to church or shelter bazaars...now that's the Christmas spirit!

Snow

Make snowflake cookies to snack on, paint white bulb ornaments to look like little snowmen and add plenty of glitter. Make mini button snowmen on cards & tags too! In place of glitter, you can use granulated sugar...when sprinkled onto glue, it dries sparkly!

Wooden eggs make silly snowmen that kids will love. Paint eggs white, add googly eyes, carrot noses and dotty smiles. Give 'em by the dozen!

Gifts from the
Kitchen

Everyone on your list will love gifts they can snack on! Try making gift mixes, decadent fudge or decorated sugar cookies. Package them in holiday tins or fancy jars and dress them up with labels, tags and ribbon.

Kid Friendly

Invite neighborhood kids over for an afternoon of easy (and fun!) crafts. Stock up on stickers, pom-poms, pipe cleaners and plenty of craft glue. They can make surprise gifts to take home for Mom & Dad!

Santa and reindeer cookies, dotted with red hots, make yummy snacks for kids of all ages. Better yet, bake up a few dozen cookies and have the neighborhood kids over to decorate them!

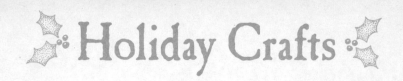

Holiday Crafts

Pepperminty Lip Balm

So cool and refreshing, everyone on your list will want some!

6 T. almond oil
2 t. honey
4 t. beeswax, grated
5 drops vitamin E oil

5 drops peppermint
   essential oil
8 1/2-oz. lidded pots

In a double boiler, melt almond oil, honey and beeswax together; remove from heat, allowing mixture to cool slightly. Add vitamin E and peppermint oils; stir until well blended. Spoon into pots and allow to cool before covering. Makes 8 pots.

Wintertime Skin Smoother

A pampering treat for when Jack Frost is nipping!

1/2 c. almond oil
1 oz. beeswax
1 T. cocoa butter

12 drops peppermint
   essential oil
12 drops vitamin E oil
3 2-oz. lidded jars

Heat almond oil, beeswax and cocoa butter in a double boiler until just melted; remove from heat. Stir in oils. Pour into jars and secure lids once cooled. Makes 3 jars.

Moisturizing Bath Salts

Liquid glycerine can be found in the soap-making aisle at the craft store...personalize bath salts with your favorite scent!

1 c. epsom salts   food coloring
1 c. baking soda   2 T. liquid glycerine
7 to 10 drops essential oil

Combine salts and baking soda, mixing well. Add essential oil and food coloring a few drops at a time until desired strength and color; add glycerin. Mix well until consistency is powdery and there are no clumps. Makes about 2 cups.

Mix & match scents and colors for heavenly bath salt combinations. Try orange and vanilla-scented layered in a pretty jar...tie on a tag with ribbon and they're ready to give.

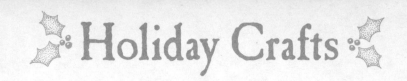

Holiday Crafts

Cozy Fleece Scarves

Everyone can bring a yard of fleece in their favorite color or pattern...you supply the decorations!

1 yd. fleece
yarn or embroidery needle
cotton yarn in contrasting
   colors

felt scraps
embroidery floss
craft glue
assorted buttons or beads

Cut fleece into 3 strips width-wise; each will be a scarf. Blanket stitch all around the edges with yarn. Cut out fun holiday shapes from felt; blanket stitch around the edges using embroidery floss. Spread craft glue liberally and evenly on back of felt shapes; place on scarves. Add buttons, beads or any other embellishment you like.

Give your scarves extra pizzazz...it's easy!
Tack on yarn fringe purchased from the craft
store or make 3-inch cuts about an inch apart
across the short end of the scarf. Tie a simple
knot in each cut piece or, for extra sparkle,
thread baubles, charms or beads onto
the fringe before knotting.

10

Easy Felt Ornaments

Use your cookie cutters for clever holiday patterns!

cookie cutters
tracing paper
scissors
felt squares

buttons, beads, felt scraps
needle & embroidery floss
polyester fiberfill
ribbon

Trace cookie cutters onto tracing paper and cut out. Using the pattern, cut two of each design from felt and add embellishments. When decorated to your liking, stitch the two felt shapes together. Use an easy running stitch and leave a small opening for stuffing. Stuff with polyester fiberfill until plump but not over-filled. Stitch opening closed and add a floss or ribbon loop for hanging.

Felt is so easy to use and is available in
a rainbow of colors...plus it's inexpensive
so stock up! Add a simple felt candy cane or
stocking appliqué to the cover of pillows for
cheery seasonal decorating.

Holiday Crafts

Wired-Up Ornaments

Once you get started on these, it's hard to stop!

wire cutters
silver 18-gauge craft wire
metal cookie cutters in
    holiday shapes

24-gauge craft wire in
    assorted colors
needle nose pliers
ribbon

Cut about a yard from the 18-gauge wire and wrap it around outside edge of the cookie cutter tightly; press wire into the curves of the cookie cutter to mold it into the same shape. This wire will be the frame of your ornament. Remove cookie cutter. Use long pieces of the multi-colored wire to wrap the framework at random. Be sure to tuck the wire ends in and twist around the frame so no loose ends poke you. Attach a length of ribbon at the top to hang.

Add some extra sparkle to your Wired-Up Ornaments...thread shimmery seed beads, silver charms or tiny jingle bells onto colored wire before wrapping it around the bigger wire frame.

Bottle Cap Push Pins & Magnets

What a clever way to add personality to a bulletin board!

bottle caps   push pins
craft glue   magnets

Turn caps upside down and add a drop of craft glue. Press the head of a push pin or a magnet into the glue and hold until secure. Continue with remaining caps. Allow to dry overnight.

Hang a cheery holiday greeting...just bend heavy wire into letter shapes! Spell out "Joy" or "Noel" and then attach fresh greenery sprigs to the wire letters with green florists' tape. Add a loop and hang from jute across a doorway or mantel.

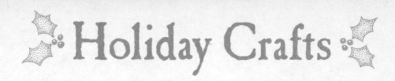

Holiday Crafts

Snow-Kissed Votives

Frosted candles are a festive Christmas gift
for anyone on your list!

glass votive holders   votive candles
silver metallic permanent
    ink markers

Wash glass votive holders with warm soapy water and dry well. Use markers to write holiday messages like "Merry Christmas" or "Ho-Ho-Ho!" You can even personalize them with a dear friend's name. Add designs like snowmen or snowflakes. Allow ink to dry well and tuck votive inside.

Look for foil stars at office supply stores... you can get hundreds of stickers for next to nothing. They're perfect to stick on purchased glass votive holders. In minutes, you can have gold-star gifts for teachers, neighbors or hand them out as favors at holiday parties!

Rolled Beeswax Candles

*Look for honeycomb sheets in the candle-making aisle
at the craft store.*

16"x8" honeycomb   hair dryer
   beeswax sheets   20" cotton wick

If the beeswax you are working with is rolled, unroll it gently.
If it's stiff or cracks while unrolling, soften it by warming with
hair dryer set on low. You can tell wax is soft enough to work
with when it's slightly sticky to the touch. Lay a piece of wick
along the short edge of the beeswax sheet, fold sheet over to
cover the wick and squeeze together. Carefully roll up the
sheet, taking care to keep edges even. Apply low heat with the
hair dryer to mold edges together; smooth the bottom to make
a flat surface on which candle can sit. Give along with a pretty
saucer to assure safe burning.

Experiment with these easy candles...heat
them slightly with a hair dryer on low heat
and roll them in glitter or flower petals. Press
in seashells, sparkly jewels or simple
thumbtacks to dress them up!

Holiday Crafts

Season's Greetings Candles

So pretty and super simple to make!

alphabet rubber stamps
& inkpad
white tissue paper
scissors

hair dryer
6 to 10" pillar candles
Optional: charms, beads,
buttons, raffia or ribbon

Stamp greetings onto tissue paper; allow to dry. Cut out words; set aside. Apply low heat to the area of the candle where you want to place the words; press tissue paper words into the warmed wax. Continue to apply heat until tissue paper becomes invisible and only the word remains. Tie on charms, buttons or beads with a little raffia or ribbon. Choose single words or 2 to 3 word phrases for the quickest crafting...try it with picture stamps too!

Look for tiny photo frame charms at the craft store. Frame a vintage Christmas image or a photo of you and a loved one and tie on to Season's Greetings Candles with a twist of raffia.

Rooftop Gift Bag

*Perfect for wrapping fudge, cookies, peanut brittle,
almond bark...gifts from the kitchen are always welcome!*

white paper lunch bag   hole punch
scissors   ribbon
colored paper   craft glue

Fill bag with your gift; fold over top. Cut a rectangle from
colored paper for the roof; fold paper over top of bag. Punch
two holes through roof and bag; thread ribbon through and tie
a bow. Cut decorative shapes from paper and glue on house to
embellish with windows, trees, a door and shutters.

Paper lunch bags are a must-have for gift
giving. Dressed up like a house (above) or with
a simple ribbon tie, they're so versatile. Try
rubber stamping them with holiday images or
words, add a snowman face to a white bag,
trim the top with decorative-edged scissors or
use a hole punch to offer a sneak peek inside.

Handmade Cards

Stitch a holiday sentiment or a jolly snowman face onto a square of vintage fabric for a one-of-a-kind greeting...use colorful embroidery floss and add beads or buttons if you like. To give, use spray adhesive to adhere fabric to cardstock.

Curl white pipe cleaners into tight spiraled circles and glue to cardstock to make a fuzzy snowman. Mini black buttons make perfect eyes and tiny twigs can be glued on for arms...how sweet!

Make a card that looks just like your front door! Cut a window in the top third of the front, draw on details and add a button for the door knob. A festive wreath is the finishing touch...your greeting goes in the window!

Use thin satiny ribbon to stitch accents onto handmade cards...threaded through sparkly beads, it'll add an elegant touch to any card.

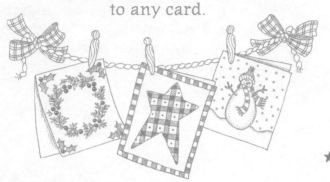

Cut 4 descending lengths of green ribbon and glue them in the shape of a Christmas tree. Better yet, stitch them on with tiny buttons...they'll look just like ornaments!

Stitch a simple feather tree design on a square of unbleached muslin. Look through Grandma's button box to find small buttons and charms to stitch on the tree as ornaments...so pretty! Use spray mount to affix muslin to cardstock or a gift bag and surprise someone special.

Gift Tag Ideas

Dress up gift tags with old buttons or fabric yo-yos. Use cookie cutters as patterns. Just trace around a snowman cookie cutter, cut out and add finishing touches!

Use glittery paint to sparkle up your cards and tags...or just sprinkle loose glitter on before ink or paint dries.

Craft a little vellum envelope and slip your gift tag inside. Before you seal it shut, add a pinch of glitter, sequins or confetti...don't forget to add your message on the back!

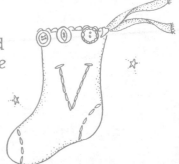

Cut a tiny felt stocking and stitch a simple initial in the center...add buttons to the top edge and tie onto pretty packages.

20

Use decorative-edged scissors and trim tags...layer them on a different color, texture or pattern paper.

Sew a simple running stitch around tags using embroidery floss for an easy border...use multiple colors and really mix it up!

While you're making stacks of tags, stamp out a roll of kraft paper for some homemade giftwrap. Each of you can take home enough for a few extra-special gifts!

Brush silk leaves with diluted gold paint for a shimmery wash of color. Allow to dry and use a metallic marker to write the name in the center. Punch a small hole near the stem and thread ribbon through for a clever tag.

21

Gift Mixes

Any-Flavor Chipper Mix

1/2 c. sugar
1/2 c. chopped nuts
1 c. any flavor chips
1 c. brown sugar, packed

2-1/2 c. all-purpose flour
1 t. baking soda
1/4 t. salt

In the order listed, layer the first 4 ingredients in a one-quart, wide-mouth jar. Sift together remaining ingredients and add to jar, packing down tightly. Secure lid and attach instructions.

Instructions:
Cream together 3/4 cup butter, one egg and one teaspoon vanilla. Stir in dry ingredients. Shape dough into one-inch balls and place on lightly greased baking sheet. Bake at 350 degrees for 12 to 15 minutes. Makes about 3 dozen.

Mmmm...GOOD! (if I do say so myself)

Copy this tag, cut it out & color to your liking... tie it onto your container for a personal touch!

Snow White Cocoa Mix

2 t. vanilla powder   1 c. white chocolate chips
2 t. orange zest   1/4 c. mini marshmallows

Combine ingredients; place in a small airtight container. Makes about 1-1/4 cups. Attach instructions below.

Instructions:
Combine 1-1/2 cups milk and 1/4 cup mix in a heavy saucepan over medium heat. Whisk well until chocolate is melted and smooth. Contains enough for 5 servings.

Jot these down on a tag of your own or use ours below. ↓

Snow White Cocoa Mix

Combine 1-1/2 cups milk and 1/4 cup mix in a heavy saucepan over medium heat. Whisk well until chocolate is melted and smooth. Contains enough for 5 servings.

Attach these instructions to this yummy cocoa mix...friends will know just how to fix it!

Sweets & Snacks

Spicy Mustard Dip

So simple and always a crowd pleaser when served with chips, pretzels and even veggies!

1 c. mayonnaise
1/2 c. sugar
1/4 c. horseradish mustard

2 t. oil
2 t. garlic powder

Combine ingredients together; cover and refrigerate 2 to 3 hours before serving. Makes about 2 cups.

Quick Mini Sausage Wraps

So fast and easy to make...they'll be gone before you know it!

3 10-oz. pkgs. mini smoked
   sausages

1 lb. bacon, sliced into thirds
1/2 c. brown sugar, packed

Wrap each sausage with a bacon piece; secure with a toothpick. Arrange in an ungreased shallow baking pan; sprinkle generously with brown sugar. Bake at 350 degrees until bacon is done, about one hour; transfer to a serving plate. Makes 30 servings.

Party-Perfect Pinwheels

*Easy to take to a get-together if you place the rolled tortillas
in a cooler and then slice them after you arrive.*

4 green onions, chopped
2 8-oz. pkgs. cream cheese,
  softened
1-oz. pkg. ranch salad
  dressing mix
5 12-inch flour tortillas
3/4 c. pimento-stuffed
  olives, chopped

3/4 c. black olives, chopped
4-1/2 oz. can chopped green
  chiles, drained
4-oz. jar chopped pimentos,
  drained
Garnish: fresh parsley,
  chopped

Combine first 3 ingredients; spread evenly over one side of
each tortilla. Stir remaining ingredients together; spoon over
cream cheese mixture. Roll up each tortilla jelly-roll style;
wrap each in plastic wrap. Refrigerate for at least 2 hours; cut
into one-inch slices and garnish with parsley. Makes about
40 servings.

Delicious Dill Dip

Serve in a bread bowl...scoop out the inside for dipping!

8-oz. pkg. cream cheese,
  softened
1 c. sour cream
1 c. mayonnaise

1/2 c. green onion, chopped
2-1/4 oz. can sliced black
  olives
1 T. dill weed

Blend together until smooth. Serves 6 to 8.

Sweets & Snacks

Speedy Peanut Butter Cookies

That's correct…there's no flour in these cookies!

1 c. sugar   1 egg
1 c. creamy peanut butter

Blend ingredients together; set aside for 5 minutes. Scoop dough with a small ice cream scoop; place 2 inches apart on ungreased baking sheets. Make a criss-cross pattern on top of each cookie using the tines of a fork; bake at 350 degrees for 10 to 12 minutes. Cool on baking sheets for 5 minutes; remove to wire rack to finish cooling. Makes 12 to 15.

White Chocolate Snack Mix

Served up in festive cups, this mix is a hit!

10-oz. pkg. mini pretzels
5 c. doughnut-shaped oat
   cereal
5 c. bite-size crispy corn
   cereal squares
2 c. salted peanuts

1 lb. candy-coated chocolate
   baking bits
2 12-oz. pkgs. white chocolate chips
3 T. oil

Toss pretzels, cereals, peanuts and chocolate baking bits together in a large mixing bowl; set aside. Melt chips and oil over low heat, stirring often; pour over cereal mixture. Mix gently; spread onto wax paper. Break apart into pieces when cool. Makes 5 quarts.

Fancy Fruit Pizza

Try it with apples, grapes, peaches, berries and bananas!

18-oz. pkg. refrigerated
   sugar cookie dough
3-oz. pkg. cream cheese,
   softened
1/3 c. brown sugar
1 c. sour cream

1/2 t. vanilla
4 c. assorted fresh fruit,
   sliced into bite-size
   pieces
1/3 c. apple jelly, melted

To form crust, press cookie dough into 12" pizza pan. Bake at 350 degrees for 10 to 15 minutes or until golden; set aside to cool. Beat together cream cheese, brown sugar, sour cream and vanilla. Spread on cooled cookie crust. Arrange sliced fruit on top and brush melted jelly over fruit. Refrigerate at least one hour before serving.

Candy canes not only taste good, they look great! Tie a bunch together with a pretty ribbon, stick a dozen in a plain clear glass or trim packages with these old-fashioned favorites. Don't just rely on good old red & white...have fun and coordinate candy canes with your giftwrap!

Sweets & Snacks

Dreamy Hot Mocha

This recipe makes enough for 4 servings...
double it for more friends!

1/4 c. chocolate syrup	Garnish: whipped cream
1-1/2 qt. strong coffee	
1 c. milk	

Place all ingredients in a medium saucepan. Heat over low heat until heated through but not boiling. Serve in mugs and top with whipped cream, if you like.

Spiced Lemonade

Served warm or cold, it's so refreshing.

1/2 c. lemon juice	1/8 t. nutmeg
1/2 c. brown sugar	1/8 t. ground cloves
1/2 t. vanilla extract	1/8 t. allspice
1/4 t. cinnamon	10 c. warm water

Add ingredients to a pitcher with a lid; shake well. Set aside to cool to room temperature. Pour through a coffee filter into another pitcher; discard solids. Makes 8 to 10 servings.

Almost-Champagne Punch

A delicious non-alcoholic version!

2-ltr. bottle club soda   6 c. white grape juice
2-ltr. bottle ginger ale

Combine ingredients in a large punch bowl. Serve in champagne glasses and toast to crafty creativity!

Try freezing bright berries or tiny wedges of lemon inside ice cubes. Drop them into refreshing drinks...fresh mint leaves are pretty too!

Craft Party Supplies

Use this helpful list as a guide for gathering supplies for your Christmas craft party!

- ☐ mailing tags
- ☐ rubber stamps & ink
- ☐ cardstock
- ☐ scrapbooking paper
- ☐ vellum

- ☐ buttons
- ☐ beads
- ☐ spools of ribbon
- ☐ charms & sequins
- ☐ pipe cleaners
- ☐ glitter
- ☐ assorted stickers

- ☐ craft glue
- ☐ hot glue gun & sticks
- ☐ florists' tape
- ☐ spray adhesive

- ☐ craft punches
- ☐ decorative-edged scissors
- ☐ pinking shears
- ☐ wire cutters
- ☐ needle-nose pliers

- ☐ craft wire
- ☐ push pins
- ☐ bottle caps
- ☐ magnets
- ☐ beeswax sheets

- ☐ yarn & sewing needles
- ☐ embroidery floss
- ☐ heavy thread
- ☐ yarn, jute or raffia
- ☐ cotton fleece
- ☐ felt squares

✓ Take-Along Checklists

Craft: _____
Supplies Needed:
☐ _____   ☐ _____
☐ _____   ☐ _____
☐ _____   ☐ _____
Other: _____

Craft: _____
Supplies Needed:
☐ _____   ☐ _____
☐ _____   ☐ _____
☐ _____   ☐ _____
Other: _____

Craft: _____
Supplies Needed:
☐ _____   ☐ _____
☐ _____   ☐ _____
☐ _____   ☐ _____
Other: _____

Fill 'em out and tote these handy checklists to the
craft store with you when shopping for your ⭐
party...you'll have everything you need!

Index